HOLIDAY HISTORY
INDEPENDENCE DAY

by Kristine Spanier, MLIS

pogo

Ideas for Parents and Teachers

Pogo Books let children practice reading informational text while introducing them to nonfiction features such as headings, labels, sidebars, maps, and diagrams, as well as a table of contents, glossary, and index.

Carefully leveled text with a strong photo match offers early fluent readers the support they need to succeed.

Before Reading

• "Walk" through the book and point out the various nonfiction features. Ask the student what purpose each feature serves.

• Look at the glossary together. Read and discuss the words.

Read the Book

• Have the child read the book independently.

• Invite him or her to list questions that arise from reading.

After Reading

• Discuss the child's questions. Talk about how he or she might find answers to those questions.

• Prompt the child to think more. Ask: Do you celebrate Independence Day? If so, what are some activities you do that day?

Pogo Books are published by Jump!
5357 Penn Avenue South
Minneapolis, MN 55419
www.jumplibrary.com

Copyright © 2024 Jump!
International copyright reserved in all countries.
No part of this book may be reproduced in any form without written permission from the publisher.

Library of Congress Cataloging-in-Publication Data

Names: Spanier, Kristine, author.
Title: Independence Day / by Kristine Spanier, MLIS.
Description: Minneapolis, MN: Jump!, Inc., [2024]
Series: Holiday history | Includes index.
Audience: Ages 7-10
Identifiers: LCCN 2022043404 (print)
LCCN 2022043405 (ebook)
ISBN 9798885244541 (hardcover)
ISBN 9798885244558 (paperback)
ISBN 9798885244565 (ebook)
Subjects: LCSH: Fourth of July–Juvenile literature.
Fourth of July celebrations–Juvenile literature.
Classification: LCC E286 .A1765 2024 (print)
LCC E286 (ebook)
DDC 394.2634–dc23/eng/20220907
LC record available at https://lccn.loc.gov/2022043404
LC ebook record available at https://lccn.loc.gov/2022043405

Editor: Jenna Gleisner
Designer: Molly Ballanger

Photo Credits: iamlukyeee/Shutterstock, cover (fireworks); Dan Thornberg/Shutterstock, cover (flag); glenda/Shutterstock, 1; 5 second Studio/Shutterstock, 3; North Wind Picture Archives/Alamy, 4; Everett Collection/SuperStock, 5; Drew Angerer/Getty, 6-7; Bettmann/Getty, 8-9; Jose Luis Pelaez Inc/Getty, 10; kali9/iStock, 11; GABRIELLE LURIE/Getty, 12-13; Robert A. Powell/Shutterstock, 14-15; shiv.mer/Shutterstock, 16; Sergii Koval/Shutterstock, 17; Richard Ellis/Alamy, 18-19; Blend Images/SuperStock, 20–21; Pixel-Shot/Shutterstock, 23.

Printed in the United States of America at Corporate Graphics in North Mankato, Minnesota.

TABLE OF CONTENTS

CHAPTER 1
A New Nation 4

CHAPTER 2
Independence Day Traditions 10

CHAPTER 3
Independence Day Around the World 16

QUICK FACTS & TOOLS
U.S. Independence Day Place of Origin 22
Quick Facts 22
Glossary 23
Index 24
To Learn More 24

CHAPTER 1

A NEW NATION

British **colonists** began moving to North America in 1606. More than 165 years later, they were still under Britain's rule. The king made them pay **taxes**. Colonists wanted freedom. The **Revolutionary War** (1775–1783) began.

Delegates met in Philadelphia, Pennsylvania. Thomas Jefferson was one. He wrote the **Declaration of Independence**. It was approved on July 4, 1776. The United States was a new nation.

Declaration of Independence

CHAPTER 1   5

The document was read in public on July 8, 1776. Some say a large bell rang afterward. It may have been the **Liberty** Bell. Today, the bell is a **symbol** of freedom. We can see it in Philadelphia!

DID YOU KNOW?

The Statue of Liberty is another symbol of freedom. The statue holds a tablet in her left arm. The tablet has a date on it. It is July 4, 1776.

CHAPTER 1

CHAPTER 1

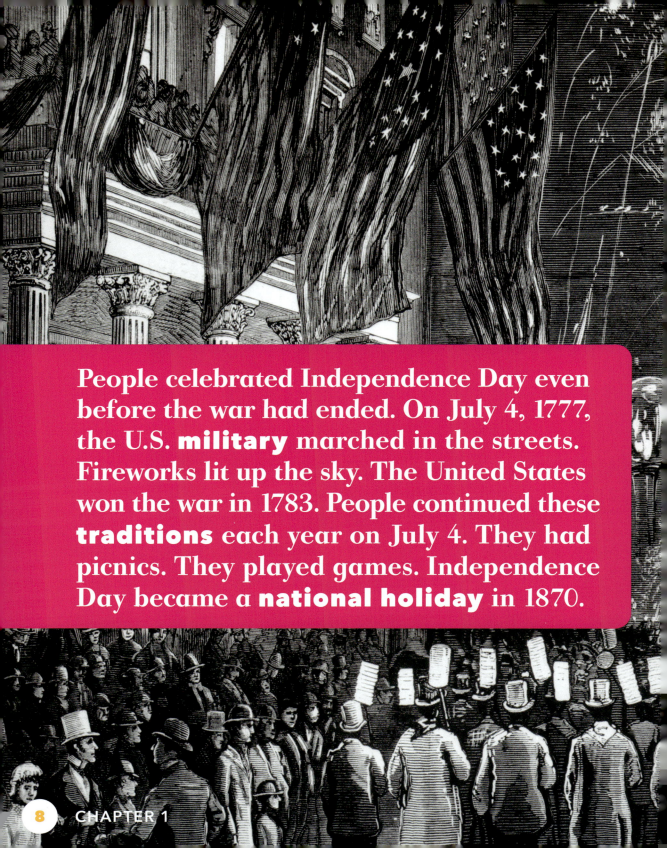

People celebrated Independence Day even before the war had ended. On July 4, 1777, the U.S. **military** marched in the streets. Fireworks lit up the sky. The United States won the war in 1783. People continued these **traditions** each year on July 4. They had picnics. They played games. Independence Day became a **national holiday** in 1870.

TAKE A LOOK!

The first American flag was made in 1777. Today's flag has the same colors, number of stripes, and meaning. But the number of stars has changed. Take a look!

1777 AMERICAN FLAG

PRESENT AMERICAN FLAG

■ = bravery   □ = **purity**   ■ = fairness

☆ = 13 colonies
≡ = 13 colonies

☆ = 50 states
≡ = 13 colonies

CHAPTER 1   9

CHAPTER 2

INDEPENDENCE DAY TRADITIONS

Today, Americans celebrate Independence Day in some of the same ways they did in the past. Many businesses close. People dress in red, white, and blue. They wear clothes with stars and stripes.

It is usually warm in July. People have picnics and barbecues outside.

Many towns and cities have parades. People line the streets to watch. They wave flags. Marching bands play.

> **WHAT DO YOU THINK?**
>
> Parades are a fun way to show national pride. They bring people together. How else could you show national pride?

CHAPTER 2

Thousands of people watch fireworks in Washington, D.C. Other cities and towns across the country have fireworks, too. People watch them light up the night sky.

WHAT DO YOU THINK?

Fireworks can be dangerous. It is against the law to buy them in some states. Do you think this is a good idea? Why or why not?

CHAPTER 3
INDEPENDENCE DAY AROUND THE WORLD

Countries around the world celebrate their own freedom. People in India celebrate on August 15. On this day in 1947, India became free from Britain. People fly kites the colors of India's flag.

kite

16 CHAPTER 3

joumou soup

Haiti became free from France in 1804. People celebrate on January 1. They make joumou soup. It is made with beef and pumpkin. It is a symbol of freedom.

CHAPTER 3

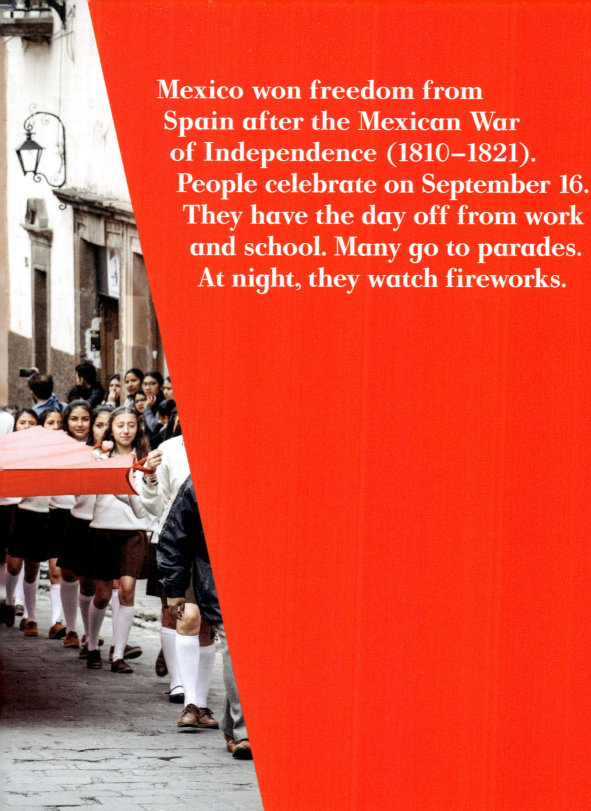

Mexico won freedom from Spain after the Mexican War of Independence (1810–1821). People celebrate on September 16. They have the day off from work and school. Many go to parades. At night, they watch fireworks.

CHAPTER 3   19

Independence Day honors freedom wherever it is celebrated. It is a day to be with friends and family. It is a time to be proud of where you live. Do you celebrate Independence Day?

CHAPTER 3

QUICK FACTS & TOOLS

U.S. INDEPENDENCE DAY PLACE OF ORIGIN

QUICK FACTS

Date: July 4

Year of Origin: 1776

Place of Origin: Philadelphia, Pennsylvania

Traditions: parades, picnics, barbecues, parties, fireworks

Common Symbols: American flag, the colors red, white, and blue, bald eagle, Statue of Liberty, fireworks, Declaration of Independence, Liberty Bell

Foods: hamburgers, hot dogs, potato salad, watermelon, lemonade, pie

GLOSSARY

colonists: People who leave one area to live in and control another.

Declaration of Independence: A document declaring the freedom of the 13 American colonies from British rule.

delegates: People who represent other people at a meeting or in a legislature.

liberty: Freedom.

military: The armed forces of a country.

national holiday: A legal holiday established by the federal laws of a nation.

purity: Freedom from immorality or wickedness.

Revolutionary War: The war in which the 13 British colonies in North America broke free from British rule and became the United States of America.

symbol: An object or design that stands for, suggests, or represents something else.

taxes: Money that people must pay in order to support a government.

traditions: Customs, ideas, or beliefs that are handed down from one generation to the next.

QUICK FACTS & TOOLS

INDEX

Britain 4, 16
colonists 4
colors 9, 10, 16
Declaration of Independence 5, 6
fireworks 8, 15, 19
flag 9, 12, 16
France 17
Haiti 17
India 16
Jefferson, Thomas 5
Liberty Bell 6
Mexican War of Independence 19
Mexico 19
North America 4
parades 12, 19
Philadelphia, Pennsylvania 5, 6
picnics 8, 11
Revolutionary War 4, 8
Spain 19
stars 9, 10
Statue of Liberty 6
stripes 9, 10
symbol 6, 17
traditions 8
United States 5, 8
Washington, D.C. 15

TO LEARN MORE

Finding more information is as easy as 1, 2, 3.

1. Go to www.factsurfer.com
2. Enter "IndependenceDay" into the search box.
3. Choose your book to see a list of websites.

QUICK FACTS & TOOLS